The Luddites: The History and Legacy of the English Rebels Who Protested against Advanced Machinery during the Industrial Revolution

By Charles River Editors

Nicolas Perez's picture of a steam engine

About Charles River Editors

Charles River Editors provides superior editing and original writing services across the digital publishing industry, with the expertise to create digital content for publishers across a vast range of subject matter. In addition to providing original digital content for third party publishers, we also republish civilization's greatest literary works, bringing them to new generations of readers via ebooks.

Sign up here to receive updates about free books as we publish them, and visit Our Kindle Author Page to browse today's free promotions and our most recently published Kindle titles.

Introduction

Marcus Schweif's picture of a spinning jenny

The Luddites

Between the 18th and early 19th centuries, Britain experienced massive leaps in technological, scientific, and economical advancement. This powerful period has since been immortalized as the great Industrial Revolution, during which Britain became a formidable force that boasted unmatched economical growth, drastic changes in living conditions, and even the emergence of a neglected social class. Vast portions of rural lands were transformed into interconnected, complex, and multitasking cities. Dozens of innovative inventions and products were churned out in bulk and sold to the masses for the first time ever. Some of the greatest thinkers and creators ventured forth from the shadows. Scientists, engineers, merchants, and manufacturers alike were at the height of their prime, nurtured by a culture that embraced the vision of growth, progress, and industrial unity.

The Industrial Revolution saw Britain rise to the top and become the envy of the world's most prestigious nations. At the same time, the pivotal era was far from perfect, featuring a dark underbelly and an army of unsung heroes.

It was American writer and futurist Alvin Toffler who once called technology "the great growing engine of change." The 18th century German linguist Johann Gottfried von Herder was another proponent of enlightenment and technological progress. "Nothing in Nature stands still," said von Herder. "Everything strives and moves forward." One would be hard-pressed to find anyone today that would disagree with these sentiments. Those whose opinions suggest otherwise are often thoughtlessly dismissed, and those who hold them ridiculed as tin-foil-hat sporting paranoids or pretentious "hipsters."

But what happens when the very instruments meant to help people begin to put lives at stake? Meet the Luddites, a 19th century brotherhood of rebels who vowed to annihilate every last one of the newfangled spinning machines that cost thousands their jobs. The Luddites' riots are indefensible, at least from the standpoint of violence, but they beg the question of whether the protests were nonsensical acts of rage carried out by thugs who sought to exploit imagined fears or desperate measures taken by those who felt neglected by the government.

The Luddites: The History and Legacy of the English Rebels Who Protested against Advanced Machinery during the Industrial Revolution chronicles the revolution and the negative reaction to it. Along with pictures of important people, places, and events, you will learn about the Luddites like never before.

The Dawn of a Revolution

Invigorated by the new financial stability and scientific progress introduced to Britain as they inched closer to the 18th century, the empire steered its attention to mending its unstable industry and strengthening its delicate economy. During this time, farming and sheep raising were the main – and in many areas, only – source of livelihood and income. At least 75% of the population consisted of farmers who struggled to make as much use as they could of the land. While the raising of animals was common and basic farming tools were readily available, efficiency in the workforce, apart from British industries as a whole, still had much room for improvement.

Before drone-shipping, instant international communication, and other creature comforts, the most basic of human interaction – including trans-town transportation outside of one's own 2 feet – was a privilege. As a result, the lives of medieval villagers were usually confined to their own towns and villages. Food was usually produced locally, and the morale of villages depended predominantly on the fruitfulness of harvesting season. Droughts, crop infestations, and overall poor harvests were unavoidable, leaving farmers and their families no choice but to brave through long and bitter winters. Goods were also produced locally, and on occasion, a few selected items were brought in from overseas. These exclusive imports, which were shipped to the London and Bristol ports, could only be afforded by those at the top of the tier. Despite the various and varied advancements in scientific progress, the bulk of the population entering the 18th century remained poorly educated. Proper education from prestigious schools or highly trained tutors was reserved for the wealthy.

The new century brought with it the development of the cottage industry, which was designed for cloth merchants to capitalize on the average farmer's downtime. If this new partnership – which normally involved the production of quality textiles from the farmer's end – was successful, it could generate higher profits for cloth merchants.

The process was as ingenious as it was straightforward. First, cloth merchants distributed raw wool to the different farming households on his team. The entire family would take part in the cloth-making process. Women scrubbed the wool clean, dipped the fabric in dye, then scraped it clean with the bristles of their sharp nail combs. The clean wool was converted into thread with a spinning wheel, and the thread woven into cloth with a loom through a grueling process that required more brawn. As such, this was a job that typically called for the men in the family.

The merchant dropped by at scheduled times and picked up the finished products before unleashing them onto the market. There was great profit to be made from this process, as merchants could sell the cheaply made products for a sweet markup. The success of the cottage industry helped in boosting the trade of the nation, which historians claim aided in preparing the nation for the impending revolution.

The thriving national trade and high demand for British product overseas were only some of the many instigators that propelled Britain into this new age of industrialization. Others point to the nation's abundant reservoirs and natural riches. As Britain traditionally opted for wood rather than coal for heat, the country bore massive deposits of the black gold, many of them untouched. Besides the availability of coal and other valuable resources, the "flexible government" brought about by the Glorious Revolution aided in the nurturing of these unorthodox ideas.

Some have also acknowledged the financial situation in Britain at the time, which played a significant role in bringing about the revolution. The newly established bank and the growing profits from the blossoming businesses funded many of these new visions and turned them into ventures. The creation of promissory notes and modern credit facilities gave the common people more money to spend. The wealthy, who were feasting upon the biggest slice of the pie, also became avid patrons of the new ideas and inventions that came their way.

By the mid-18th century, mass manufacturing in the textile industry was at its peak, which came with the overwhelming demand for more thread. In 1764, James Hargreaves made it his business to find an answer that would satisfy this swelling demand.

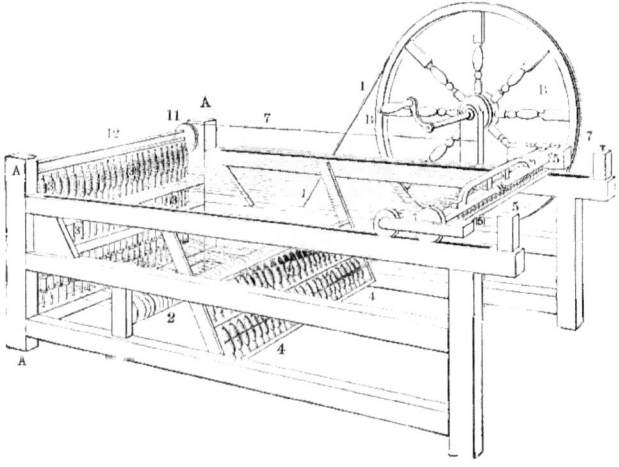

The design of the spinning jenny

Throughout the 18th century, more inventors with affinities for fabricating made more improvements upon dated technology across all the major industries. The region by the Severn River had become a hotspot for iron production. Along came the Darby family, a family of innovators soon to become the iron mavens of their era. In 1709, Abraham Darby chose to pick up from where Clemente Clerke had left off. He discovered that coke, which were essentially carbon leftovers from the "incomplete combustion" or heating of coal, could be used as an alternative to charcoal in the smelting of pig iron, a constituent of cast iron materials and products. Darby quickly patented his coke-made pig iron, and he soon began outselling other merchants with his pig iron pots, kettles, and other kitchenware.

In the late 1700s, yet another field of industry took to the limelight – machinery and tool manufacturing. One of the first figures to surface from this field was John Wilkinson. In 1761, Wilkinson and his brother inherited their father's iron furnace in Bersham. The New Bersham Company, as it was then known, became the paramount manufacturer of quality weapons, applauded for their guns, castings, and cannons.

Wilkinson

In 1774, Wilkinson, who had caught the inventing bug himself, filed a patent for a "boring engine," which would revolutionize the world of cannonry. Before the boring stage, old-fashioned cannons were first cast (the pouring of molten materials into a mold), and topped off with a core, which was an internal mold used to fill the gaps left by the cast. Wilkinson's engine, which turned the gun barrel instead, increased the precision of cannon balls and decreased its detonation rates.

The same engine was later used to bore the cylinders for Watt and Boulton's steam engines. Wilkinson's company also manufactured the cylinders and other components for the pair for 20 years. Later, Wilkinson was issued another patent for the spiral grooves he carved into cannons, which improved the distance and accuracy of cannon balls. He died rich, and was laid to rest in a handsome iron coffin.

The acme of British tool-making innovation would come in the early 19th century. Henry Maudslay, from Woolwich, Kent, was practically born to the sounds of droning drills and clanking machinery. He was sent to work at the age of 12 as a powder monkey, scooping gunpowder into cartridges for hours on end. 2 years later, he apprenticed as a blacksmith and continued to hone his building skills, and at age 18, he was enlisted to create the world's first "unpickable" lock.

What would truly put his name on the map, however, was his invention of the screw-cutting lathe. This hulking metal instrument, which produced uniform screws in huge volumes, contributed to the efficiency and ensuing triumphs of the Industrial Revolution. These lathes may have already existed before Maudslay, but his design, which included gear shifts, a slide-rest, and lead-screws, were untouchable in terms of durability and practicality.

As the 18th century drew to a close, it was clear the Industrial Revolution in Britain was now at its prime. By the end of the 1700s, Great Britain had churned out what would be worth over £2.5 billion today of locally manufactured products. Coal production had become a mammoth industry, and was on the constant rise. To put this in perspective, 2.7 million tons of coal were mined in 1700. A century later, that number had ballooned to 10 million, but it had yet to reach its climax. Another century later, that number was at 250 million.

On Christmas Eve of 1801, the residents of Camborne, England wandered out of their shops and homes, their eyes bulging in amazement. What resembled the front half of a train, perched upon a 4-wheeled wagon with steam shooting out of its bulky cylinder, appeared around the corner. As the strange locomotive chugged its way down the street, its 7 beaming passengers waved at the crowd. This curious creation was none other than Richard Trevithick's "Puffing Devil," the first "steam-powered passenger vehicle." The Devil could even climb uphill, as one of its passengers described, "like a little bird...going faster than I could walk." Regrettably, the Devil burst into flames when it overheated just a few days after its debut, but mishap aside, it seemed as if the 19th century was off to a promising start.

Chris Allen's picture of a replica of the puffing devil

The ever-growing British economy ushered in what was known as the Victorian middle-class, or as they were dubbed at the time, the "middling sort." This was a term that referred to the class of people wedged between the aristocracy and the poor of Britain. Come the 19th century, the middle-class of Britain was at its highest and most heterogeneous point yet.

Alongside the hotshot manufacturers were small-fry entrepreneurs who set up modest stalls and shops of their own, thus creating niche markets for themselves to keep from knocking heads with those in the big leagues. The increased profits obtained from across the board of British businesses aided in sponsoring the ships, railways, banks, and insurance companies of the industrial empire.

The budding middle-class reaped the benefits of their newfound prosperity. When laws were later passed to shorten working hours, people were granted more time for leisure. More and more pubs cropped up across the nation, cementing itself as a go-to socializing spot for the middle and working classes, who found it difficult to turn down their affordable menus. Time was freed up for people to complete or pursue specialized fields of studies and interests. Others dressed up for a fancy night on the town, dining in expensive restaurants and visiting theaters.

Manufacturers and merchants across Britain seized the opportunity to make use of the middling sort's new spending money. Both handwritten and printed posters, leaflets, and other pieces of Victorian advertisements were rolled out to the masses. Towards the late 19th century, advertisers only became more creative. Some dressed up their shop windows with decorative signs that highlighted their state-of-the-art products and other bestsellers. Others rented out slots on the billboards and newspapers. One poster showed a stylish and comely couple on a balcony with steaming cups of Cadbury's Cocoa Drink in hand as they peered out at the scenic view of the river below them. Another for Pears' Soap showed a pretty, plump maiden, with fair and supple skin, rinsing her hands daintily in a wash basin.

The rise of the middle-class and available spending money also helped to bring about the sudden factory boom. The factory boom also led to substantial changes in the workforce. The dwindling cottage industry forced single and married women to find work outside of their homes, the majority of them seeking out employment in factories. Most women found jobs in domestic service and textile production, and a fraction worked in coal mines.

The growth spurt that the factories and manufacturing plants in Britain experienced was like a cursed coin, one that concealed a disturbing dark side. Other than women, thousands of children were sent to work at the factories, plants, and mills. Many manufacturers even preferred children, since they were a much cheaper hire. Children were also easier to marshal, because at one point, 40% of the population in England were under the age of 16. Orphans were also preferred by employers, as they could be effortlessly whisked away and easily replaced if needed be.

As productive as these factories were, the working conditions were inconceivable. Regular shifts consisted of 12-14 hours each, and this was excluding overtime. Then, there were the wage discrepancies. On average, male workers earned about 75 pence ($62.40 USD), whereas women were paid 35 p ($29.12) and children made the equivalent of $12.48. On top of these barely livable wages, fines for the most trivial of offenses, including whistling, daydreaming, or having an extra speck of dirt on one's work station, were imposed upon them. Some workers accused their employers of manipulating the clocks so that they could be written up and fined for tardiness.

Workers were also subject to inhumane discipline, the most common being strapping, which were lashings with thick leather straps. Children were subject to their own version of horrors; those who misbehaved or failed to perform up to standards were made to wear leaded iron weights around their necks. Others were hoisted into baskets and dangled from the roof, as if to scare the work ethic into them. Some had their ears – never their fingers, lest it affect their work – nailed to the workshop tables.

Regardless of the era's pros and cons, Britain had become one of the brightest and most influential industrial powerhouses in the world. By 1835, an estimated 106,000 power looms were installed across the nation, and by 1890, it was said that 90% of all ships in the world were manufactured in Britain. In 1852, the great nation reached another milestone, celebrating over 7,000 miles of railroad tracks that weaved throughout the land.

Luddite Predecessors

"Those engines of mischief were sentenced to die,

By unanimous vote of the trade,

And Ludd who cannot a position defy,

Was the grand executioner made." - Chumbawamba, "The Triumph of General Ludd," 1988

Ned Ludd has been crowned with many titles – General, Captain, and even King Ludd – and while he is none of the above, this elusive character was and continues to be revered by anti-establishment protesters, the technologically-weary, and other nonconformists today. He did not strut around in polished silver armor or wield a shiny sword, nor did he slink around mysteriously in a hooded cape with a bow and arrow in hand. Quite the contrary, artistic depictions of the cult figure show a young, rugged-looking man sporting a loose polka-dotted smock over his tattered shirt and breeches, his unruly dark hair cinched by a headband, and his fingers wrapped around a sharpened knitting needle. He is also sometimes pictured as a burly young man, his veiny and almost comically beefy biceps bulging as he holds a mighty mallet over his head.

An 1812 engraving of the leader of the Luddites

There was apparently a time when spies and militiamen were dispatched by the government to capture this slippery mutineer, for this man, whom they call the "leader of the Luddites," was raising a violent insurrection that threatened to upset the 18th century British textile market. This hostile hoodlum, as authorities saw him, was believed to be in command of invisible, organized terror squads so vicious and unpredictable that they struck terror into even the most hardened policemen and soldiers. Sightings of Ludd, though rare, often contained sensational details, and were propagated by disconcerted mill owners, authorities, and townspeople alike. One militiaman, for instance, swore he was one of the few who spotted Ludd, albeit briefly. The militiaman claimed to have caught a glimpse of Ludd before the wily fugitive disappeared behind a corner. Ludd, he said, was a towering, strapping figure with a "ghostly white" complexion, brandishing "a pike in his hand, like a sergeant's halberd," and a sinister look in his beady eyes.

Most modern historians have since ruled out his existence, but the legends surrounding Ludd have yet to be buried, and like most legends, there are many versions of Ludd's so-called heroics.

The most popular variant is that in the year 1779, Ludd, occasionally referred to as "Edward Ludlam," was a spirited, but temperamental young apprentice to a stockinger based in Leicester. One afternoon, Ludd, who had worked overtime hours for several weeks straight sans complaints, found himself on the receiving end of his mentor's tirade. Ludd's mentor berated him for "knitting too loosely," and fired at the apprentice less-than-savory insults about his intelligence, all for failing to "square his needles." Instead of standing meekly with his eyes riveted to his boots, the apprentice's wrath grew with every drop of spittle that hit his face. Before his mentor could even complete his diatribe, a snarling Ludd snatched up the hammer next to his station and pounded the stocking frame in front of him with all the might he could muster until all that was left were battered fragments and wooden shards.

Another similar rendition of the tale takes place in Antsey, a quaint English village by Charnwood Forest. A young weaver of the same name was said to have been whipped so savagely by his employer that he seized a mallet from a fellow weaver's station and smashed a pair of newly purchased stocking frames into pieces. He then shoved his speechless employer out of the way and ventured into Sherwood Forest, choosing to live out the rest of his days in the wilderness. King Ludd was, they say, so magisterial and wise that every critter in the forest, no matter the size, bowed down before him.

Yet another interpretation of the tale characterizes Ned Ludd as an adolescent village boy, and an unpopular one at that. The boy was regarded as uncouth and uncultured, mocked mercilessly, and branded a "half-wit," one who had to rely on his brawn to support his destitute family. Ludd did his best to ignore the name-calling, but his tormentors hounded him day in and day out, so much so that he inevitably snapped. He turned on his heel and gave chase, and when he failed to catch up to them, the infuriated Ludd stormed into a weaver's house and brutally pummeled a couple of spinning frames, fragments and broken components flying in all directions. Unbeknownst to young Ludd, one of his bullies was peering into the window of the house he had broken into, and had witnessed his entire fit. Seeing what Ludd was capable of, they made certain to steer clear of him from there on out.

Rumors surrounding this intriguing Ned Ludd character eventually arrived in Nottingham. Though it seemed as if no one could produce proof of ever having met the man, Ludd became the poster child for factory employee protests, most specifically the Luddites, vilified by the public as an alleged secret society of hooligan weavers who aimed to vanquish every last one of the newfangled contraptions that posed a threat to their livelihoods. The Luddites were known to send barrages of anonymous letters to their targets prior to their attacks, and though its content was serious, they closed their documents with facetious signatures, the most common one being: "Ned Lud's Office, Sherwood Forest."

While some fancied themselves as regular Robin Hoods – crude, but selfless paladins that took from the rich to give to the poor – Ned Ludd was, at least to the Luddites, a man whose bravery outshined the Prince of Thieves himself. "Chant no more your old rhymes about bold Robin Hood," the Luddites sang as they marched. "His feats I but little admire, I will sing the achievements of General Ludd, now the hero of Nottinghamshire!" Others caroled, "They said Ned Ludd was an idiot boy, that all he could do was wreck and destroy, and he turned to his workmates and said: 'Death to machines, they tread on our future and they stamp on our dreams!'"

It is easy to dismiss the concerns of the Luddites and write them off as aggressive, narrow-minded people who staunchly refused to accept healthy technological progress, but it is easier to understand their grievances when looking at the history of textiles in England. In fact, weavers were the first in the country to be recognized as a guild in the year 1100, which enforced set standards quality-wise and regulated prices to level the playing field. The guild was also granted a charter issued by the crown that guaranteed them certain rights, liberties, and other privileges, including the right to collect taxes ("ferms"), select bailiffs, and even preside over its own court. All members forked over yearly subscription fees, which were kept in a treasury that covered medical costs, financed pensions, and whatever else its members required. As such subscription fees were unprecedented at the time, historians consider the guild of weavers to be the oldest company in London.

The weavers once sat on one of the top blocks of the totem pole, for the textile industry served as the beating heart of the medieval English economy. The power the weavers bore was so great that it intimidated the masses. Most vocal were those in the upper echelons, demanding that King John dismantle the Weavers' Guild, promising to cough up higher taxes in return to make up the difference, yet the weavers stood their ground.

Come the 14th century, the power of the Weavers' Guild wavered as they fell under the governance of the mayor. Cloth-workers, drapers, mercers, and haberdashers also came into the picture, establishing guilds of their own and further subtracting from the weavers' influence in the industry. Be that as it may, weaving remained a respected craft, and was in 1490, even issued a Grant of Arms. Weaving was then acknowledged as an "incorporated craft" in the early 1500s, and received ratification of their official ordinances later that century.

Weaving in an era prior to the introduction of advanced robotic machinery was arduous, to say the least. At the same time, it was a family affair, and a great source of pride over the discipline and skill required for the craft. As such, it was an honorable trade passed down from one generation to the next, and long before behemoth textile mills and fabric factories began to crop up by the dozens, wool and linen fabrics were produced in the homes of English working class families. These families then sent their wool to local spinners and weavers, who created cloths out of their raw fabrics with manually-operated machinery.

It was around this time that cotton and silk gradually began to enter the textile scene. Halfway into the 18th century, Derbyshire and Nottinghamshire established the kingdom's first water-powered cotton mills. Cheshire and Lancashire added color to the competition when they introduced a chain of steam-powered textile mills. Many family-based businesses were, naturally, considerably anxious about the daunting newcomers, but the majority bit the bullet and transitioned to keep up with the changing industry, swiping up the scores of jobs the newly-opened mills in their towns had to offer.

That being said, there was an adjustment period. While most still worked alongside their family members and neighbors in "teams," these former independent "outworkers" were now made to do the bidding of their employers, and worked on a schedule set by their superiors.

As one might expect, textile production, even with the help of state-of-the-art 18th century mills and equipment, was still a laborious process. For example, since cotton was not native to Britain, tightly-compressed bales of the plant were delivered to the cotton mills. First, these bales were placed onto a mesh and "willowed," which saw workers "batting" the raw cotton with sticks to dry out and separate the chunks. Secondly, the cotton was blended, to create different qualities and textures of yarns, then scutched, which entailed more cleaning, as well as fishing out cotton seeds and other foreign fibers. Next, the twisted fibers of the cotton were straightened out and smoothed between a pair of machine cards (wire teeth attached to leather or wooden boards). Following another thorough round of cleaning, the cotton threads were then stretched and twisted, priming them for bobbins, and later spun and sized.

Wool-making followed a similar, equally taxing process. Wool was derived by either shearing, extracting loose fibers directly from the back of their flocks, and fellmongering, the last of which involved plucking out the fleece from the hides of slaughtered sheep. Wool used to make stockings back in the day were predominantly sourced from dead flock. The loose wool was then graded, scoured, carded, combed, spun, and woven.

Dyeing, which had workers dunking the fabric into simmering baths of brightly colored vegetables and fruits, occurred after the cleaning of the wool. Occasionally, instead of scouring the wool, some workers opted for the more traditional approach of "fulling," which entailed soaking the wool in stale urine and beating it with a mallet-like apparatus. As repulsive as this might sound to the common man, the scouring process – which aimed to eliminate dust, burrs, grease, and other unwanted substances – was equally, if not more demanding. Scourers had to first scrub the fleece vigorously with soap, soda, and other acidic solutions, then boil and rinse them off in various receptacles, before flattening the wool and allowing it to dry under the baking heat of the sun.

The production of silk textiles in the days before the Industrial Revolution was a craft that called for even sharper finesse and attention to detail. Patterned silk cloths, for example, could only be created with a duo of skilled weavers and an arsenal of costly raw materials and equipment at one's disposal. An outline of the pattern was first mapped out by intricately threading the warp onto the loom. One of the weavers was then tasked with inserting the wefts as a "drawboy" tugged on the harness cords of the loom.

Silk weaving only secured its place as a part of the mainstream textile industry some time in the 16th century. Spitalfields was among the first to specialize in the craft before Bishopsgate, Bethnal Green, Whitechapel, and other neighboring towns pounced on the growing market. They soon formed their own guild, and was incorporated as a "London City Company" in 1629.

The double-needle knitting skill of stockingers was yet another integral component of the Victorian textile industry. The "dropped stitches" technique allowed for the 3-dimensional curves necessary for form-fitting articles of clothing, such as stockings, socks, gloves, and whatnot. The extensive training that went behind knitting these items set stockingers back a pretty penny, which made them more resistant to the mechanization of their craft as opposed to weavers and spinners.

Bearing this in mind, when William Lee of Nottinghamshire's Calverton unveiled to the world his revolutionary stocking frame in 1589, stockingers were initially skeptical, but they grew to embrace the invention. The invention itself, after all, is said to have been conceived by either Lee's jealousy at being spurned by his overworked wife. The bearded needles, which came with fishhook-like ends, were some of the stocking frame's main features. An excerpt from *Twist Collective*'s article, "Fancying Framework Knitting," illustrates how the machine works: "Using a series of treadles and plates, loops are formed by laying a thread over the stem of all of the needles. Then small metal plates are pushed between each needle until loops are formed and pushed into the hooks. The hooks close and as the carriage of needles is released, new loops are formed and pulled through the previous row of stitches...Original frames could only produce a plain stockinette stitch; any patterning had to be done by laborious reversing [sic] the stitches...They were then seamed to produce a tube that would enclose a leg, a job often done by the knitter's wife."

As implied by the passage, the invention had not deprived them of their jobs; rather, the stocking frame sped up production and reduced some of the grunt work. Stockingers in general reacted favorably to the change, and took the time to learn how to master the new machines. Framework knitting continued to be a family business, though employed by small-time bosses, or as they called them, "masters." Men operated the improved, but unwieldy frames. Their wives and eldest daughters worked alongside them, sealing stocking seams. Children were also made to help out with menial chores, such as wrapping yarn around the bobbins.

The lives of weavers, spinners, framework knitters, and other cloth makers in the textile industry were by no means a breeze. These were thankless jobs that reaped little monetary reward, often only enough to keep their heads above water. Most lacked the funds to purchase these stocking frames, and as a result, were made to rent them. Whether or not they even had orders was neither here nor there – they were still made to shell out the rental fees each month. Still, spinners, knitters, and weavers alike remained optimistic about the future of the thriving textile industry, and did their best to educate themselves about the constantly improving technology in their fields. In 1657, the Worshipful Company of Framework Knitters was incorporated in the capital.

When the very machines the textile workers were struggling to understand threatened to render their operators obsolete, the situation began to spiral out of control. In the 1660s, English silk barons in Spitalfields began to purchase machine looms in droves, prompting the loss of hundreds of jobs seemingly overnight. The fury of the hand-loom weavers, who were unceremoniously fired without warning, was exacerbated not only by the cold reality of their inability to compete with the machines, but the cries of their starving families.

In August 1675, dozens of disgruntled and unemployed hand-loom weavers took to the streets, their fists firmly clenched around bats, hammers, and axes galore. For the next three days, the revolters, clad in symbolic emerald-green aprons that supposedly paid homage to the Levelers, a political faction from the English Civil War that promoted religious tolerance and equality, terrorized the textile districts. Armed weavers hacked away at the boarded up doors of textile mills and factories, and once they had let themselves in, the establishment owners and what was left of the workers scattered. Some attempted to intervene under the orders of their cowering employers, but they could do nothing but watch as the adrenaline-fueled intruders swung away at the once-glinting machine looms, laying waste to the costly equipment. The more theatrical rioters dragged the machine looms to the street and burned them in impromptu bonfires. Also targeted by the rebels were French immigrant weavers the locals accused of stealing their jobs.

Authorities eventually regained control, but the destruction was incredibly costly, and the government was shaken by the ramifications brought about by poverty, even among traditionally docile folk such as the weavers. But unfortunately, rather than look deeper into the growing resentment of the weavers and remedying the plights of their citizens, politicians amped up security. The years that followed were punctuated by more weaver uprisings, which were extinguished with force quickly. Parliament finally began hosting negotiations in an attempt to break the toxic cycle, but the promises granted by the magistrates were no more than temporary, quick fixes. Soon enough, protesters again marched the streets.

Violence was not ideal, and it was a last resort for most, but the effectiveness of their collective and organized actions was not lost on the weavers. As such, they decided that they would subsequently tackle all their problems, be it through stern words or brute violence, as one cohesive unit.

1668 brought what is now remembered as the "Bawdy House Riots." Silk weavers fetched the green aprons in the back of their closets and poured into the streets once more, the distant echoes of the rioters' pro-liberty and anti-Parliament slogans striking fear into the spines of mill and factory owners in their paths. On the one hand, the government would have by now been fully aware that the uprisings were almost strictly triggered by economical reasons. On the other, they fretted that "radical" republicans and members of the 5th Monarchists, an extremist Puritan sect involved in multiple assassination plots, would begin to secretly puppeteer the rioting weavers' operations, if they had not done so already.

The Bawdy House Riots, like the previous insurgencies, were quashed by the army, but nevertheless, the damage inflicted was so disastrous that local textile tycoons began to slow down on the mechanization of the silk weaving industry, visibly decelerating the process for about 100 years or so. What ensued was an immediate downswing in weaver-led rebellions.

One might assume that the government began to relax, but they continued to stay vigilant and grew even more wary of the weavers. In 1683, when authorities received warnings about "distress and desperation [brewing] among the journeymen weavers" in Whitechapel, they swiftly sent over a troop of cavalrymen before the textile workers could turn hostile.

The weavers celebrated the deceleration of loom mechanization as the number of jobs available were on the ascent for the first time in decades, but what they failed to forecast was the number of foreign immigrants that would teem into England during this time, the bulk of them bright-eyed, able-bodied, and adequately skilled young men eager for a stable factory job. Not only were the local weavers now forced to vie with immigrant workers for factory jobs, they had to make do with their shrinking salaries, for out-of-town employees cost considerably less than their local counterparts. To put this into perspective, hand-loom weavers earned approximately 20 shillings a week in the 1770s, yet less than 40 years later, they were scraping by on less than 10. A loaf of bread that normally sold for 9 pence was hiked up to a shilling and 5 pence. Moreover, men were losing out to female employees and child labor, who earned far less (roughly 5 and 2 shillings a week, respectively).

The poisonous cotton dust that ate away at the lungs of factory workers and the need to develop their own lip-reading language (known as "mee-mawing" in Lancashire) due to the noise pollution made the pitifully low wages even less appealing. Furthermore, the stories of employers striking their workers with leather straps, fastening hefty iron weights around the necks of under-performing children, and tacking the ears of workers onto tables with nails as punishment were even more jarring, but they did nothing to dissuade thousands from applying from for factory jobs.

In 1771, 8 years before the legendary Ned Ludd famously lost his temper, a man named Richard Arkwright erected a factory by Cromford's River Derwent in Derbyshire to shelter his beloved spinning-frames. The entrepreneur was overjoyed at having secured the spot, which, as he boasted to his lawyer, was strategically located by "a remarkable fine stream of water...in an area full of inhabitants." English scientist, historian, and broadcaster Adam Hart-Davis elaborates on the significance of Arkwright's establishment: "[His] mill was essentially the first factory of this kind in the world. Never had people been put to work in such a well-organized way. Never had people been told to come in at a fixed time in the morning, and work all day at a prescribed task. His factories became the model for factories all over the country and all over the world..."

Arkwright

The efficient standard operating procedure Arkwright designed managed to streamline production and cause the employers' savings to rise. With the reduction in time and labor it took to produce an article of clothing, both the salaries of the factory workers and local hand-loom weavers experienced a drastic decline. Sprinkling more salt onto the wound, inventors began to make headway with automatic looms and steam-powered mills that same year. Crompton's mule, for one, called for only one skilled weaver to operate numerous machines at once.

The disoriented and jobless weavers would not maintain their composure for long. An article from *The Derby Mercury*, published in October of 1779, detailed the anxieties of authorities, who could sense the tumult that was bound to unfold: "There is some fear of the mob coming to destroy the works at Cromford, but they are well-prepared to receive them should they come here. All the gentlemen in this neighborhood being determined to defend the works, which have been of such utility to this country. 5,000 or 6,000 men can be at any time assembled in less than an hour by signals agreed upon, who are determined to defend to the very last extremity, the works, by which many hundreds of their wives and children get a decent and comfortable livelihood." Despite the 6,000 men apparently on standby, rioters succeeded in destroying more than 300 frames that week.

Six years later, inventor Edmund Cartwright of Manchester debuted an innovative power loom that could run via horses or waterwheel. Upon testing his invention in a mill he co-owned, he came across a thrilling revelation - not only could he put any unskilled boy behind the weaving machine untrained, they could churn out 3 ½ more pieces of clothing in the time it took a weaver to knit one by hand. With that, their earnings took an even deeper dive.

In 1807, a petition signed by 13,000 weavers was submitted to Parliament calling for the establishment of a set minimum wage. Much to their dismay, their petition, entitled the "Weavers' Minimum Wage Bill," failed to sway the House of Commons. In May of the following year, a rabble of 6,000 weavers gathered in Manchester's St. George's Fields to protest the absurd 8 shillings the average weaver was now earning for an 80-hour work week, and to call for a 33% increase in wages. They were forced to disband by the muscle deployed by the authorities, but the resolved protesters returned to St. George's once more the next day, this time with a mob of 15,000. The cavalrymen, or "dragoons" as they were then known, were abundantly armed but thoroughly unequipped to handle a crowd of such a size. Spooked, the nervous troops fired at the crowd recklessly, killing one and injuring dozens in the process.

The better part of the masses sympathized with the weavers, who they felt were wronged by the corrupt government and their heartless employers. A series of strikes followed suit, many of them attended by non-industry civilians, demanding justice for the slain weaver and the many others indefinitely paralyzed in the melee. Roving dragoons broke up and apprehended those involved in secret meetings on conspiracy-related charges, but this only provoked the protesting weavers further. They retaliated and lashed out by wrecking the neighborhood's most powerful factories and mills. Vandals splashed barrels of corrosive sulfuric acid (vitriol) into factory windows they had punched in, and emptied them directly over the automatic power looms, cheering as the cracking and melting machines began to smoke, as if gasping for air.

The June 7, 1808 issue of *The Times* told readers, "[A] variety of rumors have been pouring in, and are hourly increasing from the country. A number of weavers have been compelled to leave their looms, and have been deprived of their shuttles by the malcontents, rewards for the apprehension of whom have been offered by the Magistrates; the cavalry are scouring the country and general alarm prevails…The small [jail] at Rochdale, we are told, has been burnt down by them, and a few of their incarcerated brethren liberated. A respectable manufacturer at Heywood was dragged from his bed last night, and several beaten by a party of weavers…The aspect, upon the whole, is gloomy."

As it turned out, this was only the beginning.

The Ways of the Luddite

"It has becoming appallingly obvious that our technology has exceeded our humanity." – attributed to Albert Einstein

Though tensions between the weavers and textile magnates were tangibly felt throughout the country, the friction was propelled to an entirely new level during the turbulent years of the Napoleonic Wars. Between the years of 1803 and 1815, France and England were embroiled in a string of minor scrimmages and full-fledged battles, with the latter doing everything to stave off what seemed like an inevitable invasion led by Napoleon Bonaparte. The English press openly ridiculed the French emperor's stature and minimized his capabilities with satirical cartoons and articles, but everyone understood these were merely a form of gallows humor. The Duke of Wellington, who would emerge as Britain's greatest general during the wars, candidly admitted he believed Napoleon alone was worth 50,000 soldiers.

The British government responded to the escalating animosity by plumping up their army and navy, as well as constructing new fortresses and reinforcing existing defenses, and needless to say, these renovations did not come cheap. Notwithstanding the volatile economy and the vehement objections of the public, taxes surged, with the funds collected being directed towards the war effort. Over time, the fiery patriotism that marked the first years of the Napoleonic Wars began to flicker as those in the working and lower classes wrestled with soaring food prices, crushing taxes, and growing unemployment.

In November 1806, a year after the Royal Navy's decisive victory at the Battle of Trafalgar, the French unleashed the Berlin Decree, which announced their intention to sever all trade relations with Great Britain. All of France's allies were expected to do the same. In January 1807, Britain reciprocated with a rash of decrees, now known as the "Orders in Council," banning all trade with France and its allies. That decree proclaimed, "that no vessel shall be permitted to trade from one port to another, both which ports shall belong to, or be in the possession of France or her allies…the commanders of his majesty's ships of war and privateers shall be, and are hereby instructed to warn every neutral vessel coming from any such port, and destined to another such port, to discontinue her voyage…"

To make good on this, the Royal Navy formed a blockade around the continent. President Thomas Jefferson expressed his misgivings about the Orders in Council to Congress. The British, Jefferson lamented, were "now at war with nearly every nation on the Atlantic and Mediterranean seas." And so, ships from the United States and several other British allies, unwilling to jeopardize their own financial security, continued to trade with France.

Still, Great Britain paid no heed to the disapproval of its allies, and in November of that same year, the British issued another decree that prohibited locals from trading with any other European port. Even more controversial was the stipulation that allowed Britain to conduct searches and confiscate goods from ships that insisted upon trading with France. This risky move, which verged on self-sabotage, backfired, because rather than strong-arming former comrades into opposing the French, the British succeeded only in isolating themselves further. Napoleon responded in kind with the Milan Decree, which granted France the right to seize any ships that did business with British merchants.

The locals, especially the poor, were affected most severely by the feuding governments. As food became increasingly scarce and prices increasingly outrageous, more and more began to loot food stores, granaries, and flour mills, and as factory jobs continued to dwindle, men queued up to enlist, desperate for the few shillings they received in compensation (about 3 shillings and 8 pence for ensigns, and 4 shillings and 8 pence for infantry lieutenants), lest they leave their families starving. With all the men gone, factories saw an immediate increase in women and child laborers.

The Napoleonic Wars raged on, and though it felt to the impoverished that the world was crashing down around them, life went on. Thanks to Arkwright's water-frame, Hargreaves' spinning jenny, Crompton's spinning mule, and the other inventions that aimed to automate the textile industry, England led the race in cloth-manufacturing and factory efficiency. In 1813, about 2,400 automatic looms were reported to be in use, but by 1850, there were over 250,000 in the country. Similarly, there were about 250,000 cotton hand-loom weavers in 1826, but just 24 years later, that number had plunged to 40,000.

The improved productivity nearly doubled Britain's profits on imports, going from £10 million to £19 million in just a decade's time, and exports, which averaged £13 million, rose to £25 million. The British government, however, did not see a single pence from the blossoming industries, as its consistently growing annual expenditures outpaced profits. The national debt stood at £106 million in 1792, and by 1814, it was at £885 million in the red.

The country also welcomed an additional 5 million immigrants during this time. The foreigners became scapegoats for many, accused of hogging the limited pool of jobs. Weavers were highly displeased with all the corners employers appeared to be cutting, and they were especially alarmed by the ghastly treatment of child laborers. These little ones – some as young as 4 – came in handy because their size allowed them to squeeze under the looms to wipe them down or take care of snapped threads. Close to 1,000 children were said to have perished in Cheshire's Quarry Bank Cotton Mill between 1785 and 1847 alone. Worse yet, they were made to endure the same 14 ½-hour work days for about a third of the adults' paychecks.

Many young apprentices deserted mills in the dead of the night, fleeing from the inhumane working environment and endless abuse. Employers released flyers advertising cash prizes in exchange for their runaway employees. A notice calling for the capture of 14-year-old Esther Price and 13-year-old Thomas Priestly, two of the 100 or so workers who escaped from Quarry Bank, read, "Whoever will apprehend the said apprentices, and give information thereof...shall receive one guinea (21 shillings) reward and be paid all reasonable expenses..." When Esther was found and dragged back to the mill, her employer whipped her, snipped off her hair, and locked her in a windowless room after work from there on out.

It was one thing to impart such abuse on adults, but subjecting children to such atrocities was another thing altogether. Textile workers badgered authorities with more petitions, only to be met with empty promises and more inaction. Farmers were also becoming agitated, for lush and rolling stretches of farmland were now occupied by factories and mills. All the while, wages continued to fall, and the number of jobs available remained stagnant. "Give us back our commons," the masses cried. "And we will do without relief!" Furious weavers and cotton workers complained, "Our troubles began with the war with France, when the law that fixed the minimum wage and the law that fixed the price of provisions according to the rate of wages, and the law that limited the employment of apprentices, were all abrogated."

Once purses were turned inside out, working class families had no choice but to take loans with high interests and pay by credit. Even then, those privileged enough to be employed brooked their own set of problems. Union-like meetings crawled with government spies, making it impossible for workers to properly discuss ways to improve their situation. If masters violated their contracts with their employees, they received a slap on the wrist, but if employees were to breach the contract, they were instantly tossed behind bars.

To the weavers, the world was against them. In fact, even the courts seemed to have betrayed them. The Protection of Stocking Frames, issued in 1788, increased fines for the "deliberate" destruction of mechanical looms and charged perpetrators with 7-14-year "transportation" sentences. It was among the most contested Acts of Parliament. Not only were those who disposed of stolen stocking frames deported to Australia, those who knowingly bought the stolen merchandise would also face imprisonment.

The Luddite movement was conceived along with the first spate of weaver-led protests and riots in the 17th century, but it was only in mid-March of 1811 that a formal name was formed. Textile mill bosses in Arnold, Nottingham received the first batch of letters from "General Ludd and the Army of Redressers" in the early months of that year. The Luddites waited, but when their letters went unanswered for weeks on end, what was left of their patience swiftly dissipated.

On the eve of March 11th, a band of freshly-unemployed weavers jimmied their way into the neighborhood's most prominent textile mills, destroying a total of 63 new machines in just a matter of hours. For the next three weeks, more of Arnold's textile mills were attacked; another 200 stocking frames lay in ruins. The disorder and panic rose to such a degree that authorities dispatched more than 400 "special constables" to guard potential targets. A whopping £50 (roughly £3,939.50 in purchasing power today) was offered by the Prince Regent to anyone who could "[give] information on any person or persons wickedly breaking the frames." Staggering cash rewards of £1,000 (£78,790 today) and higher were offered by factory owners themselves. The vandals, or as the press dubbed them, "the Luddites," were emblazoned on the front pages of national newspapers for weeks.

On the cloudy and chilly evening of November 4th, the sleepy neighboring village of Bulwell, a group of about a dozen Luddites, some with coal dust smeared all over their faces and others with scarves pulled up to their eyes, emerged from the shadows. Following a "military-style" countdown, the group proceeded towards the home of a weaver by the name of Edward Hollingsworth, their "hammers, axes, pistols, swords, firelocks, and other offensive weapons" gleaming under the moonlight. Upon their arrival, the intruders quietly surrounded the hosiery mill next to the Hollingsworth home as a lookout posted himself nearby.

In the bedchamber of the Hollingsworth manor, Edward and his wife awoke with a start. They shuffled over to their window and peered down at the commotion, watching in horror as the thugs prized the bars off the mill's windows and barged into the front door. They alerted their servants at once, but when they spilled out to the scene, the group was long gone, and at least six of the new frames had been destroyed.

The security that the group had been greeted by was so lax that they returned to the Hollingsworth estate in less than a week, and they didn't bother changing any part of their plan. Hollingsworth, however, had anticipated this, and now he was ready for them. From that point forward, at least seven of Hollingsworth's men would be stationed outside of the mill, each armed with muskets and ammunition. Even if the Luddites did manage to make it past the guards, they would only be met by a handful of the mill's oldest equipment, for the rest were safely stowed away in a storage unit about two towns over.

Hollingsworth's guards caught the Luddites by surprise, but they demanded Hollingsworth to surrender his frames all the same. When Hollingsworth refused, the Luddites and factory guards charged towards one another, with triggers repeatedly yanked on both sides. A young Luddite named John Westley, who was attempting to "[tear] down the window shutters [of the mill] to obtain entrance by force," was literally caught in the crossfire. According to local legends, Westley waved off his accomplices and urged them towards safety. As he crumpled to the floor, staining the earth with his blood, he poignantly proclaimed, "Proceed, my brave fellows, I die with a willing heart!"

Hollingsworth and his men cheered boisterously as the Luddites scooped up Westley's lifeless body and stole into the woods, but their celebrations soon proved to be premature. Once the Luddites had regrouped about an hour later, they returned, each kindled by "a fury irresistible by the force opposed to them." The Luddites kicked down the door of the mill, suppressed the guards, and wrecked every last one of the frames in sight. Their perspectives blinded by rage, the Luddites turned their attention to the Hollingsworth home, slashing up all the furniture and later setting the manor ablaze. The quick-footed Luddites then sped off in all directions. They were never identified, and that same evening, another 12 frames were destroyed by elusive Luddites in the town of Kimberly, which only gave the textile bosses in the area more reason to panic.

On the 13th of November, a swarm of about 100 Luddites set out from The Hut, an alehouse in Arnold, and headed for the town of Sutton in South London, which was, as the Luddites claimed, "a great center for manufacture of 'cut-ups' (products of inferior quality) and payment in 'truck.'" More than 300 toted rifles and muskets of varying sizes, while the rest carried hammers, pikes, cleavers, and axes. The Luddites encircled the mill of hosier Francis Betts, the foremost "principal weaver" in town, and when he failed to comply with the ultimatum presented to him, the Luddites smashed each and every one of his frames to bits. The Luddites then continued onward, burning and batting at least 70 frames in total that night. Their raucous chants haunted factory owners and uninvolved civilians alike. "Roll up Ned Ludd's family!" sang the Luddites. Those attacked despaired at their losses, but none so much as poor Betts, who was so traumatized by the experience that he lost his mind and died soon thereafter, "deranged" and financially ruined. As one might expect, with a crowd of such a size, the Luddites were bound to slip up. Around 8-12 of them were apprehended, and four of them – Gervas Marshall, John Bradbury, John Clarke, and George Green – were made to stand trial.

A 19th century engraving of Luddites destroying a machine

A few from the English weavers' community denounced what they called "needless violence," but their voices were muffled by the overwhelming majority who were tired of passivity. Branches of Luddites gradually materialized in all sizes across the country, most of them assembling in weaver-friendly taverns and other secluded bars in their villages. Another 100 frames were destroyed by the Luddites in the final week of November 1811, and another 50 in December. "There is an outrageous spirit of tumult and riot," warned the magistrates in Nottingham. "Houses are broken into by armed men, many stocking frames are destroyed, the lives of opposers [sic] are threatened, arms are seized, haystacks are fired, and private property destroyed..."

Strongly-worded posters decrying the "crimes" of textile factories and workshops were fixed onto the front doors of these establishments. Usually included in the Luddite posters were comprehensive lists of their demands, as well as consequences, should the employers fail to meet the said demands of "Ned Ludd's Army." These posters, for the most part, were enough to persuade business owners into retrieving their hand-looms from storage, but a few chose to carry on with business as is.

William Radcliffe, a cotton clothier based in Lancashire's Stockport, was among those who chose to hold down the fort. The firstthree3 months of 1812 may have been marked by an increasing number of raids targeting textile tycoons in his neck of the woods, but Radcliffe appeared unaffected. If anything, his grip around his automatic looms tightened, or at least until the 20th of March. An article from the *The Manchester Gazette* described what followed: "On Monday afternoon, a large body, not less than 2,000, commenced an attack on the discharge of a pistol, which appeared to have been the signal; vollies of stones were thrown, and the windows smashed to atoms; the internal part of the building being guarded, a musket was discharged in the hope of intimidating and dispersing the assailants. In a very short time, the effects were too shockingly seen in the death of 3, and it is said, about 10 wounded..."

About a week later, the factory and home of Emanuel Burton in Middleton suffered a similar fate. As reported by *The Leeds Mercury*, "A body of men, consisting of from 1 to 200, some of them armed with muskets with fixed bayonets, and others with colliers' picks, who marched into the village in procession, and joined the rioters. At the head of the armed banditti, a man of straw was carried, representing the renowned General Ludd whose standard bearer waved a...red flag."

With the movement now in full swing, factory owners fortified their mills and workshops. Iron bars were added to windows and the locks to all doors upgraded. Guards, who worked in rotating shifts, monitored the premises all 24 hours of the day. They were trained to alert the rest of the security team about any suspicious activities, and often fired their muskets at the first sign of trouble.

In the early months of 1812, 120 Luddites surrounded a mill in Middleton and promptly broke down the doors "with a fearful crash...[much] like the felling of great trees." The factory owner was startled, but he was also prepared. Guards rose from their crouching positions and hurled enormous stones off the rooftop as snipers attempted to gun down the rest of the intruders. At least four of the Luddites were shot dead.

Authorities exerted every effort to unmask the Luddites, but try as they might, they only managed to catch tens out of the thousands, and the spies they sent to investigate the tight-lipped Luddites fared no better. The divide between the rich and the poor was wider than ever, with the bulk of those who subscribed to anti-elitist ideologies openly expressing their support for the Luddites. "Almost every creature of the lower order both in town and country are on their side," one local official noted morosely.

More and more knitters in the East Midlands began to participate in the movement around the same time. Wages in the area had hit an all-time low, with hand-knitters now only making about 7 shillings a week, and those who managed this miserable income were the lucky ones, for the majority were only able to secure part-time jobs, if any at all. Thousands were forced to seek assistance from their local parishes, as well as the Overseers of the Poor, but no matter their intentions, these establishments could only provide them with so much. In early 1812, as many as 13,350 were receiving aid from local support groups in Nottingham alone. Meanwhile, over 1,000 royal soldiers were roaming the streets of Nottingham at a time, accompanied by another 800 soldiers on horseback, and yet the Luddites, whose loyalty to one another seemed impenetrable, persevered. The paranoia of clothiers continued to rise, with some inflating monetary prizes for information about the Luddites and others marshaling more guards. One manufacturer invested 1 shilling for every dozen of his 3,000 frames each day to ensure the safety of his property.

Contrary to popular belief, not all Luddites exhibited the same levels of criminality. Though the weavers in Leicestershire bore equal weights of hardship on their shoulders, most opted to torment their enemies with non-violent vandalism. The Luddites in Leicestershire preferred to avoid confrontation, electing instead to sneak into hosiery mills and fiddling with the jack wires of stocking frames. Such adjustments caused irritating hiccups in production, but they could be quickly fixed if located, which some Luddites felt was an adequate lesson.

Furthermore, the Luddites prided themselves on being reasonable until wronged, and most of their attacks came after a warning of some fashion. To start, a few members of the group would approach mill owners to address their problems and make an attempt to negotiate. The Luddites' general stance was that the problem lay not in the machinery, but those who purchased them. The Luddite negotiators suggested that the factory owners share the profits they were now swimming in by taxing the cloth, and these collected taxes could them serve as a rainy-day fund of sorts for the part-time and unemployed. Others proposed a deceleration in the introduction of the new machinery. They encouraged factory owners to purchase said machines in phases, rather than in bulk, to allow employees the opportunity to train for a new trade. Some employers showed compassion and worked with the Luddite negotiators to find a middle ground, but most laughed the Luddites out the door.

If the factory owners failed to cooperate, the Luddites would then proceed to drafting anonymous letters, leaflets, and posters that warned the mills to dispose of their "obnoxious frames." Once again, they campaigned for an increase in wages, and for contemptible employers to put a halt to the cut-ups and "botched work" produced by automatic looms, which they deemed dishonorable to their trade. One such letter from General Ludd ominously exhorted Henry of Leicester to be on the alert: "It having been presented to me that you are one of those damned miscreants who deligh [sic] in distressing and bringing to poverty those poore, unhappy, and much injured men called 'Stocking-makers,'; now be it known unto you that I have this day issued orders for your being shot through the body with a Leden Ball..."

Another letter from the general reads:

"Gentlemen all,

"Ned Ludd's Compliments...hopes you will give a trifle toward supporting his Army as he well understands the Art of breaking obnoxious frames. If you comply with this it will be well, if not I shall come upon you myself."

Most Luddite ambushes adhered to a similar pattern. Luddites always cloaked themselves in heavy disguises, usually by darkening their faces with charcoal and soot. Some even dressed in women's clothing, donning scraggly long wigs and dramatic makeup. They aptly referred to themselves as "General Ludd's Wives."

The most frequently used weapons among the Luddites were metal sledgehammers, which the brotherhood nicknamed "Enoch's hammers." The muse behind this moniker was the hammer's creator, blacksmith and Marsden native, Enoch Taylor. The irony of Taylor's pioneering work in the field of automatic looms and frames was not lost on the weavers. "Enoch made them," the Luddites bellowed. "And Enoch shall break them!"

For the most part, the Luddite ambushes usually destroyed only the machines, leaving the rest of the factory's interior intact. These raids also burst into the homes of factory owners to disassemble their personal spinners and weaving machines, if necessary. The number of lookouts depended on the size of the intruding party, and once their mission was complete, party leaders blasted a shot into the air and thundered, "Ned Ludd!" That was the signal for the Luddites to disperse.

Owing to the rigorous training they committed themselves to in the weeks leading up to the attack, the Luddites acted quickly and methodically, with the best of them able to deconstruct a frame in mere minutes. They were as cautious as they were physically fit, and they were almost always able to outrun anyone who tried to pursue them before vanishing into the night.

Most of the Luddites' daily drills occurred after midnight in abandoned moors, deserted industrial buildings, and isolated clearings deep in the woods, but a few claim to have witnessed these gatherings in broad daylight. One letter placed a group of Luddites by the border of Lancashire and Cheshire on the 14th of June, 1812, just shy of Ashton-under-Lyne. The witness, who was supposedly attending morning services at his local church at the time, was stunned to see more than 500 Luddites by the hillside between Ashton and Mottram. Following the deafening blast of a gunshot, a standard-bearer raised a scarlet flag, marking the start of the drills, which lasted for about 20 minutes.

Obviously, those who belonged to the lower classes had a better chance at scoring a place within the Luddite community. However, the required passion, fidelity, and unbreakable commitment that such membership entailed were not for everyone. Indeed, the initiation ceremony itself was enough to elicit second thoughts from even the toughest weaver on the block. First, initiates were blindfolded and escorted to an off-the-grid location in the fringes of town, its exact coordinates known only by the 10 elders present, each one of their faces concealed by a burlap sack. The blindfold was then removed, and the initiate was made to recite the following oath of secrecy: "I, [insert name], of my own voluntary will, do declare, and solemnly swear that I never will reveal to any person...under the canopy of heaven the names of the persons who compose this Secret Committee, their proceedings, meeting, places of abode, dress, features, connections, or anything else that might lead to a discovery of [the brotherhood]...under the penalty of being sent out of the world by the first brother who shall meet me, and my name and character blotted out of existence...never to be remembered but with contempt and abhorrence...and I further now...swear that I will use my best endeavors to punish by death any traitor...should any rise up amongst us...So help me God, and bless me to keep this my oath inviolable." Initiates were then handed a leather-bound Christian bible, and they planted a kiss on it in a rite they called the "Kissing of the Book."

On the 1st of May, 1812, Reverend William Hay of Ashton forwarded to the Home Office another round of letters detailing what he claimed to be the secret hand signals of the Luddites. Hay wrote, "The right thumb in the right waistcoat armhole, the right heel in the center of the left hoot with the toe turned square – the countersign is the reverse of this...There is another – the right-hand little finger in the mouth with the thumb pointed out, the fingers doubled. The answer is a left-hand rubbing the chin between the from [sic] and 2 first fingers."

The Luddites in Yorkshire

"As the liberty lads o'er the sea,

Bought their freedom, and cheaply, with blood,

So we, boys, we,

Shall die fighting or live free,

And down with all kings but King Ludd!" - Lord Byron, "Song for the Luddites" (1816)

Manchester, one of the foremost leaders in the field of cotton-weaving, soon became a magnet for Luddite activity. Since the mills and workshops here were much larger than that of their neighboring regions, Luddite raids were fiercer in terms of both size and destruction. From Manchester, the meteoric flames of the movement spread to Lancashire, Cheshire, and Flintshire, and by early 1812, the Luddites had flattened thousands of frames, averaging about 175 a month in the Midlands.

Even these depraved assaults were nothing in comparison to the Luddites' stint in Yorkshire. Like Manchester, factory bosses and clothiers in Yorkshire's West Riding were connoisseurs of wool, and like the locals of Manchester, those in Yorkshire suffered poverty, unemployment, and starvation, leading them to embrace the Luddite movement. The movement in the county took on many variants, but the sector led by the cloth dressers, known as "croppers," was by far the most active. Croppers were those primarily involved in cutting cloth delivered by fulling mills, and the last stages of cloth production, i.e., brushing, shearing, pressing, and so forth. The job of a cropper was not without its toil and monotony. They hovered over their work stations with 4-foot-long handheld shears weighing about 50 pounds a pair, manually trimming and ironing out pieces of "fulled" woolen cloth.

Their chief nemesis were shearing frames, or "rotary shearing machines," developed by Samuel Dorr back in 1794, which came with a "wheel of knives" that could cut multiple squares of cloth at a time. This very invention is said to be the inspiration behind the lawnmower. The cloths produced by Dorr's shearing machine were substandard, but all that seemed to matter to the profit-hungry employers were savings and increased mass production. Gig mills, which housed a fraudulent and therefore illegal type of machinery that manipulated the "naps" on woolen fabrics, also threatened to put the croppers out of work. One cropper moaned, "Now gigs and shearing frames are like to become general, if they are allowed to go on, many hundreds of us will be out of bread!"

The Luddite attacks in Yorkshire began in January 1812. They started small, preying on modest to medium-sized cropping shops in random spots across the county, but as the movement began to pick up momentum, Luddites began to set their sights on the biggest fish in the pond. By April, the Yorkshirian Luddites were bold enough to pounce on the most prestigious cropping companies, with some even looting the homes and private properties of mill owners and making off with muskets, bullets, and other valuable treasures.

With the situation intensifying at an alarming rate, the government could no longer stand idly by. They fought the Luddites' unpredictable tactics with an impetuous, but belligerent plan designed to oppress them. A total of anywhere between 12,000 and 14,400 troops deployed to Nottinghamshire, Lancashire, and Yorkshire, otherwise known as the "Luddite Triangle" or the "Luddite Trifecta." The government also managed to muster together a voluntary militia (a precursor of the Territorial Army) of some 20,000 strong, as well as a division of "special constables" that reported directly to the magistrates. A passage from a year-end report reads, "By May, it was said, Bolton had 400 special constables making rounds every night, usually armed; Salford, a suburb of Manchester, had 1,500 (10% of the male population); Manchester itself had 4,000; and Nottingham had around 1,000."

In a bid to amplify awareness and strengthen public participation, authorities enticed civilians with incentives, and even offered packaged deals to Luddites who agreed to identify themselves and "renounce their oath to General Ludd."

When even these failed to produce the results authorities so urgently desired, the government decided to up the ante. Previously, the maximum penalty for the intentional destruction of frames was a 14-year exile to Australia, but on the 27th of February, the House of Commons published a bill entitled the "Destruction of Stocking-Frames, etc. Act 1812." Pursuant to this bill, the destruction of stocking and lace frames became a capital offense.

In a surprising turn of events, when authorities convened in the House of Lords the following March for the second reading, Lord George Gordon Byron took the podium in defense of the Luddites. Byron, who would go on to become one of Britain's most famous poets, criticized Prime Minister Spencer Perceval and the politician's lackluster "efforts in the House of Lords," and his impassioned and powerful speech deprived the lawmakers in attendance of theirs. The Luddites' malevolence, Byron insisted, "had arisen from circumstances of the most unparalleled distress...The perseverance of these miserable men in their proceedings, tends to prove that nothing but absolute want could have driven a large and once honest and industrious body of...people into the commission of excesses so hazardous to themselves, their families, and the community..." To pass such a bill, said Byron, would be to value human life "at something less than the price of a stocking-frame."

Perceval

Lord Byron

Much to the consternation of Lord Byron and the Luddites, the government refused to budge from its position and published the Frame-Breaking Act as is. Four months later, the British government issued another decree that sentenced all those who took on "illegal oaths" straight to the gallows. The magistrates also vested themselves with the power to insert themselves into any premises and conduct searches at their own judgment.

With these acts in place, authorities expected to see a decline in Luddite activity, but the Luddites remained bent on rebellion, taking the Act as an open invitation for war. The number of weapons brought into raids promptly multiplied. The rioting Luddites often sang, "You might as well be hung for death as breaking a machine." They reiterated their sentiments in another brief, but potent letter that they mailed to the authorities shortly thereafter. It read, "We will never lay down arms until the House of Commons passes an Act to put down all machinery hurtful to [the common people,] and repeal that [law] to hang Frame-Breakers..."

The Luddite movement reached its climax on the 11th of April, 1812. At the stroke of midnight, a group of 150 Luddites led by 23-year-old cropper George Meller marched towards the Rawfields (Rawfolds) Mill, owned by William Cartwright of Yorkshire's Liversedge. The intruders were determined to take apart the 50 water-powered shearing frames that sloughed off 4-5 croppers each. The four-story mill was soon hemmed in by hatchet, musket, and spear-wielding Luddites, the front rows beating down the front door with sledgehammers and pelting rocks and boulders at the windows. Fortunately for Cartwright, his paranoia – aggravated by the growing and worsening horror stories of Luddite attacks in and outside of town – bore more fruit than anyone else around him expected. As the story goes, Cartwright, along with 10 other workers who had set up camp within the factory, reached for their weapons at once. As 10 of the 11 defenders shot at the intruders, the last sounded a bell that Cartwright had installed just a few days prior, which summoned the cavalry lingering nearby.

The entire structure of Rawfields Mill was enveloped by a thick, grayish fog as both parties fired at the other for a dreadful 20 minutes. The wails and grunts of collapsing men filled the air, but the Luddites refused to stand down. "Bang up, my lads!" Mellor boomed over the gunfire, waving spiritedly at those hammering away at the front door of the mill. "In with you – kill every one of them!" On the opposite side of the threshold, Cartwright's men created a barricade with every single piece of furniture that wasn't riveted to the floor.

Cartwright's plan was to tire out the intruders, a strategy that ultimately proved effective. The Luddites eventually began to slow down, and upon hearing the pounding hooves of the cavalry in the distance, Mellor and his men retreated, leaving the resilient door of the mill badly bruised but intact. The wounded limped along behind them, all but John Booth and Samuel Hartley, who lay themselves just a few feet away from the mill and awaited death. Still, the Luddites showed no remorse, even when teetering on the brink of death. When the arriving dragoons ordered Booth and Hartley to surrender the names of their accomplices, they said nothing, and when they did, they danced around their interrogators' questions. A clergyman was then sent to extract a confession from them. While Booth supposedly exhibited a hint of regret, his lips remained sealed. Suddenly, the shivering man beckoned the clergyman forward, and asked him, "Can you keep a secret?" Nodding keenly, the clergyman leaned towards him. "So can I," croaked Booth with a sly smile. He died just moments later.

Several other Luddites who were wounded in the chaos also expired from their injuries in the days that followed. Out of all the mill's defenders, on the other hand, Cartwright was the only one to suffer any injuries. The star of his celebrity brightened threefold overnight, especially among governmental officials and fellow factory owners, who viewed him as a beacon of hope in a world overrun by the Luddites.

Authorities praised Cartwright for his valiance and his ability to think on his feet. They encouraged the press to broadcast Cartwright's victory, banking on this being the deterrent that would finally convince the Luddites to head for the hills for good. As it turned out, they could not have been more mistaken, because the Luddites did not take kindly to their own blood being spilled, and they were now resolved to exact their revenge. The epidemic of assaults that followed would be unlike any other, for they were no longer geared towards the machines, but the crooks.

William Horsfall, the owner of a wool mill in the Yorkshirian village of Marsden, was one such character. Not only was Horsfall a staunch proponent of the automation and industrialization of Great Britain, the well-heeled businessman, who employed over 400, condemned the Luddites to anyone who would spare him an ear. He would give anything, he declared, "to ride up to his stirrups in Luddite blood."

Whether or not he had intended to, Horsfall became a prime target. The Luddites in the community stalked his every move, recording his routines and distinctive habits and tracking his daily routes. On the 28th of April, about two weeks after the showdown at Rawfields Mill, the Luddites pounced. Huddled behind the bushes by a road in Huddersfield's Crosland Moor district were four Luddites named George Mellor, Thomas Smith, William Thorpe, and Benjamin Walker. The men waited as the oblivious Horsfall ushered his stallion down the quiet path. At the final number of Mellor's countdown, the men cocked their rifles and lunged forth, firing several rounds at Horsfall until a fatal bullet pierced him through the groin. Horsfall fell from his horse and hit the ground with a thud, gurgling in pain as he struggled with the pistol in his holster. By the time his bloody hands managed to grip his gun, the Luddites had vanished.

This road in Crosland Moor was not particularly remote, but Horsfall's reputation among the poor and the working class was reportedly so abysmal that travelers simply trotted past him. A police report about the incident noted, "After being wounded the inhumuan [sic] populace surrounding him reproached him with having been the oppressor of the poor – they did not offer assistance. Nor did anyone attempt to pursue or secure the assassins who were seen to retire to an adjoining wood." It was only when another wool manufacturer chanced upon him that Horsfall was finally assisted. He was taken to the Warren House Inn, but the doctor they summoned could do nothing for him. He died 38 hours later.

The local government sprang into action at once, starting a purge of sorts. Even with the £2,000 reward that authorities were offering, it took nearly 8 months of painstaking investigation, furtive spying, ruthless grilling, and barbaric torture before Huddersfield magistrate Joseph Radcliffe finally located the suspects. Among the 100 or so men that were rounded up – some actual Luddites, some innocent, and some guilty by association – 64 were tried in a "Special Commission" at the York Assizes. The widely publicized "show trial" commenced on the 2nd of January, 1813, and though the proceedings only formally concluded 10 days later, George Mellor, Thomas Smith, and William Thorpe were sentenced to death on the 8th of January for Horsfall's murder. All three of them, branded the "ringleaders" of the Yorkshire Luddite movement, were just a few months shy of their 24th birthdays. Their corpses were then sent to York County Hospital, where they would be dissected in the name of "medical science."

Naturally, authorities were eager to make an example out of the Luddites. On the 16th of January, a throng of Yorkshirian civilians watched as another 14 Luddites – among them Nathan Hoyle, John Hill, John Odgen, Joseph Crowther, Thomas Brook, William Hartley, and brothers James and Job Hey – were shepherded towards the gallows. Accused of the raid in Rawfields

Mill and various other charges pertaining to firearm theft, the men were led across a field as they sang the Methodist hymn "Behold the Savior of Mankind":

> "Behold the Savior of mankind,
>
> Nailed to the shameful tree,
>
> How vast the love that him inclined,
>
> To bleed and die for thee!"

The Luddite Legacy

"One machine can do the work of 50 ordinary men. No machine can do the work of 1 extraordinary man." – Elbert Hubbard

The attack on William Horsfall is widely considered the event that marked the end of the final wave of Luddite attacks, but attacks linked to the secret society occurred sporadically in the years that followed. In 1817, Jeremiah Brandreth, a Sutton-in-Ashfield native and stockinger by trade whose connections with the Luddites dated back to 1811, was arrested for having allegedly led what is now referred to as the "Pentrich Rising." As maintained by Brandreth, in May of that fateful year, he was approached by William Oliver, who claimed to be a Luddite from London. Oliver, said Brandreth, tipped him off about a mass revolt that the Luddite chapter in the capital was planning, and urged him to assemble an army of his own.

Thus, on the 9th of June, Brandreth and the 400 men he had rallied set off for Nottingham, flaunting pikes, pistols, and bats. Upon arriving at the assembly point, Brandreth, who expected to see Oliver and his men, were accosted by royal soldiers instead. The crowd quickly dissolved, but Brandreth and 35 other men were arrested and charged with high treason. 11 of these men were deported to Australia, while Brandreth and two others were doomed to the gallows, with their bodies to be drawn and beheaded. Their decapitated heads were then paraded around the platform by the executioners.

Before they were executed, Brandreth and the other convicts cursed Oliver, labeling him an "agent provocateur" for Home Secretary Lord Sidmouth. These allegations were later examined by multiple experts and public figures, among them the poet Percy Shelley, as well as Edward Baines, a Parliament member and editor of the *Leeds Mercury*. Baines later published a gripping exposé that compiled the treasury of incriminating evidence against Sidmouth and Oliver, calling the latter "a prototype of Lucifer, whose distinguishing characteristic is, first to tempt and then to destroy." Though the Pentrich Rising had more to do with the wildly unpopular Corn Laws that resulted in unaffordable bread for the masses, it was considered by many historians to be the last major Luddite act.

Lord Sidmouth

Baines

Later that year, James Towle, who was accused of the attack against Loughborough Mill the previous June, was also marched to his death. The victim of this rogue Luddite branch was John Heathcoat, owner of the Loughborough Mill and inventor of a novel lace-making machine known as the "bobbin net frame." Heathcoat's guards attempted to fend off the 17 attackers, but they were overpowered, resulting in the destruction of 55 bobbin net frames worth about £10,000. Stocks of expensive fine lace were also reduced to ashes. Despite the fact there were 71 witnesses who backed Towle's alibi, he was found guilty by the jury, and he was hanged in Nottingham in August of 1817. The *Leicester Journal* painted a vivid picture of the grim event: "At 12 o'clock, [Towle] was brought upon the platform...where he evinced a manly and becoming fortitude, worthy of a better fate. He bowed on his entrance to the populace, but made no address. After the Chaplain had gone through the usual prayers, the prisoner gave out and sang the hymn with great solemnity and a very audible voice after which...he was launched into eternity and appeared to die without struggle or emotion..."

Towle's fidelity to the Luddites, much like his composure, was unflinching, but the same could not be said for the rest of the alleged perpetrators. The following January, one of the arrested surrendered the names of a dozen other participants, among them James Towle, the younger brother of the accused ringleader. James, found guilty of "firing a pistol at John Asher, one of the workmen in the palace, with intent to kill him," and seven others were hanged before a crowd of 15,000.

Though the violent Luddite riots eventually petered out, their ideas remained very much alive. The suffering citizens who felt neglected by their overseers continued to challenge the authorities, organizing both peaceful protests and aggressive revolutions to demonstrate their discontent with government policies. The Swing Riots, which transpired between 1830 and 1832, is thought by many to be a lesser-known agricultural arm of the Luddite movement. For 24 months, farmers, cattle herders, and ranch-hands raised hell in eastern and southern Britain, destroying hundreds of threshing machines and maiming dozens of cattle in Maulden, Bedfordshire, and Flitwick. All in all, the damage inflicted was estimated to be worth about £121,600. A report from the Poor Law Commissioners elaborated on the specifics: "Arson damage...damage - £100,000; industrial machines (Luddism) - £13,000; agricultural machines (Swing) - £8,000; riot damage - £600." Ultimately, 1,976 separate trials were conducted, which resulted in the execution of 252 rioters, as well as the temporary and permanent deportation of 505 and 233, respectively, and the imprisonment of 644 men.

Hard as it may be to believe, there was a silver lining in all of this. A few years later, the Poor Law Commissioners published the "1834 Poor Law Amendment Act," followed by the "Tithe Communication Act" in 1836. Though the wage increase was only enforced in 1850 (going from a minimum weekly wage of 8 shillings and 11 pence in 1795 to 9 shillings and 6 pence), and little progress was made in terms of working environments, this brought British workers one step closer to the fair wages and employment security that they had sought for so long.

Today, the movement is kept alive by its descendants, who call themselves the "Neo-Luddites." An excerpt from a *Gizmodo* article sums up the diversity of the culture today: "Defining 'Neo-Luddism' is...fraught. The term – and ideology – overlaps and confuses itself with a diverse collection of causes and 'isms': anti-materialism, minimalism, anarchism, eco-terrorism, anarchy-primitivism, dystopian futurology." Activist Chellis Glendinning, author of "Notes Toward a Neo-Luddite Manifesto," adds: "[The Neo-Luddites] are not anti-technology, but was against technology that was materialistic or destructive of community."

200 years later, readers can find subtle elements of the movement in a wide array of works, from the thought-provoking writings of Henry David Thoreau to the deranged ramblings in the manifesto of the "Unabomber," Ted Kaczynski. Like so many other things in life, Luddism is open to interpretation.

Online Resources

Other books about British history by Charles River Editors

Other books about the Industrial Revolution on Amazon

Further Reading

Editors, L. L. (2012). Yorkshire Luddism – Timeline. Retrieved May 3, 2018, from http://ludditelink.org.uk/perch/resources/yorkshire-luddism-timeline1.pdf

Staggs, M. (2015, July 17). Ned Ludd, the Luddites, and a Response to Robot Alarmism. Retrieved May 3, 2018, from http://www.signature-reads.com/2015/07/ned-ludd-the-luddites-and-a-response-to-robot-alarmism/

Editors, E. (2008). Luddites. Retrieved May 3, 2018, from https://www.encyclopedia.com/history/modern-europe/british-and-irish-history/luddites#B

Editors, L. K. (2017, March 23). 10 Facts about Luddites. Retrieved May 3, 2018, from https://lessknownfacts.com/10-facts-about-luddites/

Editors, L. 2. (2014). Who Were The Luddites? Retrieved May 3, 2018, from http://www.luddites200.org.uk/theLuddites.html

Coren, M. J. (2017, April 30). Luddites have been getting a bad rap for 200 years. But, turns out, they were right. Retrieved May 3, 2018, from https://qz.com/968692/luddites-have-been-getting-a-bad-rap-for-200-years-but-turns-out-they-were-right/

Conniff, R. (2011, March). What the Luddites Really Fought Against. Retrieved May 3, 2018, from https://www.smithsonianmag.com/history/what-the-luddites-really-fought-against-264412/

Moore, A. (2012, July 18). The Luddites. Retrieved May 3, 2018, from http://www.intriguing-history.com/the-luddites/

Editors, H. C. (2016, September 1). History Documentary: The History of the Luddite Movement, The Luddites, Documentary -- The Historian Channel. Retrieved May 3, 2018, from http://historianchannel.blogspot.tw/2016/09/history-documentary-history-of-luddite.html

Editors, E. A. (2014). The Luddites' War on Industry. Retrieved May 3, 2018, from http://www.eco-action.org/dod/no6/luddites.htm

Editors, H. H. (2016, January 12). Luddism in Yorkshire: A chronology. Retrieved May 3, 2018, from http://www.historyhome.co.uk/c-eight/c-eight/distress/ludchron.htm

Bloy, M., PhD. (2005, December 30). The Luddites 1811-1816. Retrieved May 3, 2018, from http://www.victorianweb.org/history/riots/luddites.html

Editors, E. T. (2013, January 8). 1813: The Yorkshire Luddites, for murdering William Horsfall. Retrieved May 3, 2018, from http://www.executedtoday.com/2013/01/08/1813-yorkshire-luddites-william-horsfall/

Pattern, D. (2015, December 17). William Horsfall (1770-1812). Retrieved May 3, 2018, from https://huddersfield.exposed/wiki/William_Horsfall_(1770-1812)

Editors, C. E. (2016, January 11). THE LUDDITES AND THE SWING RIOTS, 1812-1832. Retrieved May 3, 2018, from https://blogs.carleton.edu/hist235/2016/01/11/the-luddites-and-the-swing-riots-1812-1832/

Kiberd, R. (2015, January 28). Burn It All Down: A Guide to Neo-Luddism. Retrieved May 3, 2018, from https://gizmodo.com/the-many-faces-of-neo-luddism-1682139778

Appleyard, B. (2014, August 29). The new Luddites: Why former digital prophets are turning against tech. Retrieved May 3, 2018, from https://www.newstatesman.com/sci-tech/2014/08/new-luddites-why-former-digital-prophets-are-turning-against-tech

Editors, H. H. (2016, January 12). A Luddite Oath: 1812. Retrieved May 3, 2018, from http://www.historyhome.co.uk/c-eight/distress/oath.htm

Editors, L. B. (2012, June 14). 14th June 1812: Luddites drill in the daytime near Ashton-under-Lyne. Retrieved May 3, 2018, from http://ludditebicentenary.blogspot.tw/2012/06/14th-june-1812-luddites-drill-in.html

Editors, D. P. (2018, February 19). THE LUDDITES. Retrieved May 3, 2018, from http://www.diptyqueparis-memento.com/en/the-luddites/

Editors, A. H. (2017). Luddites. Retrieved May 3, 2018, from https://aes-humanities8.wikispaces.com/luddites

Editors, L. B. (2012, May 1). 1st May 1812: William Hay informs the Home Office about recent threatening letters & the Luddite oath. Retrieved May 3, 2018, from http://ludditebicentenary.blogspot.tw/2012/05/1st-may-1812-william-hay-informs-home.html

Martin, J. (2017). The Myths of Ned Ludd. Retrieved May 3, 2018, from http://ludditelink.org.uk/ludditeproj3.php

Martin, J. (2017). The Myth Of Ned Ludd. Retrieved May 3, 2018, from http://ludditelink.org.uk/perch/resources/ludditelinkpdf1.pdf

D'Avolio, L. (2015, November 2). The Surprising Story of The Original Luddite. Retrieved May 3, 2018, from http://thehealthcareblog.com/blog/2015/11/02/the-surprising-story-of-the-original-luddite/

Editors, F. B. (2011, December 14). Ned Ludd. Retrieved May 3, 2018, from https://ferrebeekeeper.wordpress.com/2011/12/14/ned-ludd/

Porter, M. (2012, February 27). Who was Ned Ludd? Retrieved May 3, 2018, from http://thesnufkin.blogspot.tw/2012/02/who-was-ned-ludd.html

Safire, W. (1998, December 6). On Language; Return of The Luddites. Retrieved May 3, 2018, from https://www.nytimes.com/1998/12/06/magazine/on-language-return-of-the-luddites.html

Porter, I. (2016, August 22). Introduction to the Ned Ludd Story of Anstey. Retrieved May 3, 2018, from https://ansteylibrary.com/2016/08/22/introduction-to-the-ned-ludd-story-of-anstey-by-ian-porter/

Editors, E. (2004). Luddites Destroy Woolen Machines. Retrieved May 3, 2018, from https://www.encyclopedia.com/history/encyclopedias-almanacs-transcripts-and-maps/luddites-destroy-woolen-machines

Andrews, E. (2015, August 7). Who were the Luddites? Retrieved May 4, 2018, from https://www.history.com/news/ask-history/who-were-the-luddites

Wilde, R. (2017, September 18). Textiles During the Industrial Revolution. Retrieved May 4, 2018, from https://www.thoughtco.com/textiles-during-the-industrial-revolution-1221644

Editors, W. C. (2017). In The Beginning. Retrieved May 4, 2018, from http://www.weavers.org.uk/history

Editors, F. S. (2014, September 8). England Textile Occupations Silk, Cotton, Weaving (National Institute). Retrieved May 4, 2018, from https://www.familysearch.org/wiki/en/England_Textile_Occupations_Silk,_Cotton,_Weaving_(National_Institute)

Hopley, C. (2006, July 29). British Textiles Clothe the World. Retrieved May 4, 2018, from https://britishheritage.com/british-textiles-clothe-the-world/

Editors, A. H. (2018, February). Pre-industrial Wool and Weaving. Retrieved May 4, 2018, from https://axminsterheritage.org/wp/wp-content/uploads/2018/02/wool-and-weaving.pdf

Watt, M. (2003, October). Textile Production in Europe: Silk, 1600–1800. Retrieved May 4, 2018, from https://www.metmuseum.org/toah/hd/txt_s/hd_txt_s.htm

Ellis, F. (2015). Fancying Framework Knitting. Retrieved May 4, 2018, from http://www.twistcollective.com/collection/35-articles/features/1668-fancying-framework-knitting

Editors, G. (2015, July 16). Knitters, Framework Knitters and Stockingers. Retrieved May 4, 2018, from https://www.geni.com/projects/Knitters-Framework-Knitters-and-Stockingers/30079

Ashley, I. (2012, November 10). Bold Defiance! The Spitalfields Silk Weavers: London's 17th Century Luddites? Retrieved May 4, 2018, from https://www.indymedia.org.uk/en/2012/10/501147.html

Editors, E. N. (2016). TO GIVE ENGLAND THE POWER OF COTTON. Retrieved May 4, 2018, from https://erenow.com/modern/the-most-powerful-idea-in-the-world/11.php

Editors, B. (2014). Working conditions in factories. Retrieved May 4, 2018, from http://www.bbc.co.uk/schools/gcsebitesize/history/shp/britishsociety/livingworkingconditionsrev1.shtml

Simkin, J. (2016, December). The Luddites: 1775-1825 (Classroom Activity). Retrieved May 4, 2018, from http://spartacus-educational.com/ExamIR6.htm

Simkin, J. (2016, December). The Luddites. Retrieved May 4, 2018, from http://spartacus-educational.com/PRluddites.htm

Editors, O. U. (2014). The Industrial Revolution. Retrieved May 7, 2018, from https://www.oup.com.au/__data/assets/pdf_file/0021/58071/Oxford-Big-Ideas-Geography-History-9-ch5-Industrial-revolution.pdf

Editors, M. L. (2017). The Triumph Of General Ludd Lyrics. Retrieved May 7, 2018, from http://www.metrolyrics.com/the-triumph-of-general-ludd-lyrics-chumbawamba.html

Editors, S. A. (2016). Origin of the Stocking Frame. Retrieved May 7, 2018, from https://www.scientificamerican.com/article/origin-of-the-stocking-frame/

Editors, P. B. (2016, August 8). Today in London's radical history: 4 day silkweavers' riot against machine looms erupts, 1675. Retrieved May 7, 2018, from https://pasttenseblog.wordpress.com/2016/08/08/today-in-londons-radical-history-4-day-silkweavers-riot-against-machine-looms-erupts-1675/

Editors, E. B. (2016, March 17). Leveler. Retrieved May 7, 2018, from https://www.britannica.com/event/Leveler-English-history

Simmons, K. (2017). The Violent Face of Futurism: Fifth Monarchists or Fifth Monarchy Men. Retrieved May 7, 2018, from http://www.preteristcentral.com/The Violent Face of Futurism - Fifth Monarchists or Fifth Monarchy Men.html

Editors, M. T. (2016, June). The Fall of the Weavers. Retrieved May 7, 2018, from http://www.heywoodhistory.com/2016/06/fall-of-weavers.html

Szczerba, R. J. (2015, February 9). 20 Great Technology Quotes To Inspire, Amaze, And Amuse. Retrieved May 7, 2018, from https://www.forbes.com/sites/robertszczerba/2015/02/09/20-great-technology-quotes-to-inspire-amaze-and-amuse/#255b907d16a6

Howes, A. (2017, May 3). Were more troops sent to quash the Luddites than to fight Napoleon? Retrieved May 7, 2018, from https://medium.com/@antonhowes/were-more-troops-sent-to-quash-the-luddites-than-to-fight-napoleon-233c802c216d

Mather, R. (2014, May 15). The impact of the Napoleonic Wars in Britain. Retrieved May 7, 2018, from https://www.bl.uk/romantics-and-victorians/articles/the-impact-of-the-napoleonic-wars-in-britain

Everts, W. W. (2014). THE EFFECTS OF THE NAPOLEONIC WARS ON GREAT BRITAIN. Retrieved May 7, 2018, from http://journals.sagepub.com/doi/pdf/10.1177/003463731901600404

Editors, C. U. (2018, January 22). FRENCH AND NAPOLEONIC WARS – IMPACT ON BRITAIN. Retrieved May 7, 2018, from https://blogs.carleton.edu/hist235/2018/01/22/french-and-napoleonic-wars-impact-on-britain/

Editors, C. R. (2018). The impact of the Napoleonic wars. Retrieved May 7, 2018, from http://crossref-it.info/textguide/persuasion/33/2297

Wagner, D. (Ed.). (2016, May 26). 1807 Thomas Jefferson - British Orders in Council. Retrieved May 7, 2018, from http://www.stateoftheunionhistory.com/2016/05/1807-thomas-jefferson-british-orders-in.html

Editors, W. W. (2015). Orders in Council (January 7, 1807; November 11, 1807). Retrieved May 7, 2018, from http://what-when-how.com/the-american-economy/orders-in-council-january-7-1807-november-11-1807/

Editors, P. P. (2017, May 24). Food Riots and Recession in Napoleonic-era England. Retrieved May 7, 2018, from https://penandpension.com/2017/05/24/food-riots-and-recession-in-napoleonic-era-england/

Coke, D. P. (2018). Protection of Stocking Frames, etc. Act 1788. Retrieved May 7, 2018, from https://alchetron.com/Protection-of-Stocking-Frames,-etc.-Act-1788

Meis, M. (2013, January 16). RAGE AGAINST THE MACHINE. Retrieved May 7, 2018, from https://thesmartset.com/article01161301/

Editors, L. (2016). Luddism in the East Midlands. Retrieved May 8, 2018, from http://www.loughborough.co.uk/history/luddite.htm

Thompson, C. (2017, January). When Robots Take All of Our Jobs, Remember the Luddites. Retrieved May 8, 2018, from https://www.smithsonianmag.com/innovation/when-robots-take-jobs-remember-luddites-180961423/

Editors, L. C. (2016, October 13). Who were the Luddites? Retrieved May 8, 2018, from https://libcom.org/history/who-were-luddites

Editors, G. L. (2010, June 27). The Aims and Accomplishments of Luddism. Retrieved May 8, 2018, from https://greatlakeswimmer.wordpress.com/2010/06/27/the-aims-and-accomplishments-of-luddism/

Editors, B. C. (2017). Responses to the Industrial Revolution. Retrieved May 8, 2018, from https://webs.bcp.org/sites/vcleary/modernworldhistorytextbook/industrialrevolution/responsestoIR.html

Editors, N. G. (2017). British Army Pay Rates. Retrieved May 8, 2018, from http://www.napoleonguide.com/ukwages.htm

Editors, O. D. (2017). £1 in 1800 → £78.79 in 2017. Retrieved May 8, 2018, from https://www.officialdata.org/1800-GBP-in-2017?amount=1

Robbins, C. (2014, October 30). What is a Luddite? Retrieved May 8, 2018, from https://middleclasstech.wordpress.com/2014/10/30/what-is-a-luddite/

Editors, W. L. (2012, February 22). Luddites were not backward looking. Retrieved May 8, 2018, from https://www.workersliberty.org/story/2012/02/22/luddites-were-not-backward-looking

Editors, L. B. (2011, November 13). 13th November 1811: Mass Luddite attack at Sutton-in-Ashfield. Retrieved May 8, 2018, from http://ludditebicentenary.blogspot.tw/2011/11/13th-november-1811-mass-luddite-attack.html

Editors, L. B. (2012, April 11). 11th April 1812: Mass Luddite attack on William Cartwright's Mill at Rawfolds, near Cleckheaton. Retrieved May 8, 2018, from http://ludditebicentenary.blogspot.tw/2012/04/11th-april-1812-mass-luddite-attack-on.html

Binfield, K. (2011, April 22). Luddites and Luddism History. Retrieved May 8, 2018, from http://www.rebelnet.gr/articles/view/Luddites-and-Luddism-History

Editors, C. R. (2001, Spring). Marching With "General Ludd": Machine Breaking in the Industrial Revolution. Retrieved May 8, 2018, from http://www.crf-usa.org/bill-of-rights-in-action/bria-17-2-b-marching-with-general-ludd-machine-breaking-in-the-industrial-revolution

Editors, A. L. (2017). The Luddites War on Industry: A story of machine smashing and spies. Retrieved May 8, 2018, from https://theanarchistlibrary.org/library/do-or-die-the-luddites-war-on-industry-a-story-of-machine-smashing-and-spies

Editors, W. H. (2012, April 30). LUDDITE WOMEN. Retrieved May 8, 2018, from https://womenshistorynetwork.org/luddite-women/

Editors, U. C. (2012, April 11). Rage against the machine. Retrieved May 8, 2018, from http://www.cam.ac.uk/research/news/rage-against-the-machine

Editors, H. H. (2008, November). William Horsfall. Retrieved May 8, 2018, from https://huddersfieldhistory.files.wordpress.com/2008/11/luddite-trail-leaflet-final.pdf

Editors, B. (2008, April 24). Brontes of Haworth. Retrieved May 8, 2018, from http://www.bbc.co.uk/bradford/content/articles/2006/05/19/shirley_country_feature.shtml

Editors, Y. A. (2013, January). York and the Luddites 1813. Retrieved May 8, 2018, from https://yorkalternativehistory.wordpress.com/write-it/york-and-the-luddites-1813/

Editors, L. B. (2013, January 16). 16th January 1813: The 14 convicted Luddites are executed at York Castle. Retrieved May 8, 2018, from http://ludditebicentenary.blogspot.tw/2013/01/16th-january-1813-14-convicted-luddites.html

Editors, H. B. (2013, July 18). THE LUDDITES. Retrieved May 8, 2018, from https://historicalbritain.org/tag/frame-breaking-act/

Long, T. (2008, February 27). FEB. 27, 1812: RAGE, RAGE AGAINST THE INDUSTRIAL AGE. Retrieved May 8, 2018, from https://www.wired.com/2008/02/dayintech-0227/

Eschner, K. (2017, February 27). Byron Was One of the Few Prominent Defenders of the Luddites. Retrieved May 8, 2018, from https://www.smithsonianmag.com/smart-news/byron-was-one-few-prominent-defenders-luddites-180962248/

Editors, L. 2. (2015). Lord Byrons Speech. Retrieved May 8, 2018, from
http://www.luddites200.org.uk/LordByronspeech.html

Editors, I. S. (2013, February 27). Lord Byron and the Luddites. Retrieved May 8, 2018, from
https://infostory.com/2013/02/27/lord-byron-and-the-luddites/

Editors, W. N. (2017). Cloth-dresser. Retrieved May 8, 2018, from
https://www.wordnik.com/words/cloth-dresser

McNamara, R. (2017, May 31). Luddites. Retrieved May 8, 2018, from
https://www.thoughtco.com/luddites-definition-1773333

Editors, A. H. (2017). 1838 Parsons's Patent Model of a Cloth Shearing Machine. Retrieved
May 8, 2018, from http://americanhistory.si.edu/collections/search/object/nmah_1071046

Editors, S. M. (2016). Carpet shearing machine, c 1832. Retrieved May 8, 2018, from
https://collection.sciencemuseum.org.uk/objects/co44540/carpet-shearing-machine-c-1832-
machines-shears-textiles

Wesley, S. (2015). Behold the Savior of Mankind. Retrieved May 8, 2018, from
https://hymnary.org/text/behold_the_savior_of_mankind

Kowalczyk, P. (2018, January 5). 50 most popular technology quotes. Retrieved May 8, 2018,
from https://ebookfriendly.com/best-technology-quotes/

Simkin, J. (2015, April). Jeremiah Brandreth. Retrieved May 8, 2018, from http://spartacus-
educational.com/PRbrandreth.htm

Editors, P. R. (2017, March). Jeremiah Brandreth – the 'Nottingham Captain'. Retrieved May
8, 2018, from http://pentrichrevolution.org.uk/pdfs/Newsletter-2-The-Nottingham-Captain-
v2.pdf

Watson, G. (2017, June 13). Spies, lies and fake news - England's 'last revolution'. Retrieved
May 8, 2018, from http://www.bbc.com/news/uk-england-derbyshire-40119222

Editors, K. T. (2017). John Heathcoat (1783 - 1861). Retrieved May 8, 2018, from
http://www.knittingtogether.org.uk/behind-the-scenes/the-people/john-heathcoat-1783-1861/

Cox, M. (2017, August 29). Luddites attack factory honoured. Retrieved May 8, 2018, from
https://www.loughboroughecho.net/news/local-news/luddites-attack-factory-honoured-13510345

Editors, H. V. (2018, March 25). 1830 Agricultural "Swing" Riots. Retrieved May 8, 2018,
from http://www.hungerfordvirtualmuseum.co.uk/index.php/9-events/37-1830-agricultural-
swing-riots

Editors, H. H. (2017, January 13). Rural Unrest in the 1830s: The "Swing" riots. Retrieved May 8, 2018, from http://www.historyhome.co.uk/peel/ruralife/swing.htm

Editors, H. P. (2014, February 21). Inspiring Quotes From The Age Of Enlightenment. Retrieved May 8, 2018, from https://www.huffingtonpost.com/2014/02/21/enlightenment-spiritual-quotes_n_4817902.html?slideshow=true#gallery/338221/14

Peel, F. (2013). *The Rising of the Luddites: Chartists and Plug-Drawers*. Routledge.

Free Books by Charles River Editors

We have brand new titles available for free most days of the week. To see which of our titles are currently free, click on this link.

Discounted Books by Charles River Editors

We have titles at a discount price of just 99 cents everyday. To see which of our titles are currently 99 cents, click on this link.

Printed in Great Britain
by Amazon

19998797R00031